A Boy Named BECKONING

THE TRUE STORY OF DR. CARLOS MONTEZUMA, NATIVE AMERICAN HERO

adapted and illustrated by

GINA CAPALDI

Carolrhoda Books • Minneapolis • New York

To Mom and Cory, the most noble and fiery spirits I've ever known.
Many thanks and the utmost respect to editor Jean Reynolds...
especially for her guidance and vision. —GC

———◆———

The Yavapai people are known for their exceptional woven baskets,
one of which is represented on the opposite page. A traditional design
is a black center surrounded by stylized representations of animals and
people in an orderly pattern symbolizing the harmony of life.

———◆———

The images in this book are used with the permission of:

Sharlot Hall Museum Photo, Prescott, AZ, p. 4; Library of Congress, pp. 8 (LC-USZC4-5673), 17
bottom (LC-USZC4-5612); National Anthropological Archives/Smithsonian Institution, pp. 11
(06702500), 12 top (06716600), 12 bottom (06701800), 15 (06701900), 25 top (06702600), 25 bottom
(06702700), 27 top (06703400), 27 bottom (06700100), 29 (06702900); National Parks Service, p. 17
top; Buffalo Bill Historical Center, Cody, WY, p. 20 top; Chicago History Museum, pp. 20 bottom, 30.

Cover photo: National Anthropological Archives/Smithsonian Institution (06702600).

———◆———

Carolrhoda Books
A division of Lerner Publishing Group, Inc.
241 First Avenue North
Minneapolis, MN 55401 U.S.A.

Website address: www.lernerbooks.com

Library of Congress Cataloging-in-Publication Data

Capaldi, Gina.
    A boy named Beckoning : the true story of Dr. Carlos Montezuma, Native American hero /
adapted and illustrated by Gina Capaldi.
        p.   cm.
    Includes bibliographical references.
    ISBN 978–0–8225–7644–0 (lib. bdg. : alk. paper)
    1. Montezuma, Carlos, 1866-1923—Juvenile literature. 2. Yavapai Indians—Biography—
Juvenile literature. 3. Indians of North America—Southwest, New—Biography. I. Title.
E99.Y5M65325 2008
970.004'97—dc22   2007021745

Manufactured in the United States of America
4 5 6 7 8 9 – DP – 14 13 12 11 10 09

Author's Note

---◆---

*This story is a testament to the character, heart, and human spirit of one
extraordinary man—Dr. Carlos Montezuma.*

In a time in U.S. history when there was little or no regard for Native Americans, a
young boy named Wassaja was brutally ripped from his people to be sold into slavery.
Despite great obstacles, that boy grew up to become Dr. Carlos Montezuma—one of the
most highly respected Native Americans of his day. He wore many hats: medical doctor,
lecturer, professor, researcher, and publisher. But his most important role was that of Native
American civil rights activist. Dr. Montezuma worked tirelessly to reform the way the U.S.
government treated Native Americans. He fought for his people's right to vote and their
right to keep their ancestral land—but above all, he fought for their dignity.

This story of Dr. Montezuma's life is based on a five-page letter he wrote to Professor
H. W. Holmes of the Smithsonian Institution in 1905 in response to the professor's request for
the story of his life. Professor Holmes was gathering material on Native Americans for a
forthcoming book.

Montezuma would later reveal other, more complete versions of his life through
interviews, newspaper and magazine articles, speeches, and letters—all of which have
been saved in various libraries in museums throughout the United States. These documents
were my source for Dr. Montezuma's own words, which I interwove into the original letter
to more fully present the doctor's life. I have made every effort to be true to the original
sources and have only added brief phrases to make the text flow smoothly.

—GC

Yavapai Family Dwelling

The Yavapai Indians have lived in central and western Arizona for centuries. In the days that they roamed the deserts of the Southwest, the men were mainly hunters and gatherers and the women were known for their intricate woven baskets. This photo shows a Yavapai family in the 1880s.

When Dr. Montezuma wrote this letter to Professor Holmes, he stated that he was an Apache. Years later, he came to learn that he was not Apache but Yavapai. The direct descendants of the group from which Wassaja was taken now live on their ancestral land, known as Fort McDowell Yavapai Nation in Arizona.

October 7, 1905
Prof. H. W. Holmes
Smithsonian Institute,
Washington, D.C.

My dear friend,

I know that you are gathering information on me and what befell my people. I am, therefore, delighted to answer your questions. I hope that what I write will add knowledge, acceptance and understanding for all.

I am a full-blooded American* Indian, born in 1866 near Fish Canyon Creek in the Arizona Territory. Until the time I was five years old I was called Wassaja which means "beckoning." My people, a band of about one hundred and fifty souls, roamed the red earth plateaus. We searched for food and lived in small grass huts called oo-wahs. Life was safe and simple in my grandfather's day. It was deadly and dangerous in mine, for we had many enemies. . . .

The Awful Night at Iron Peak Plateau

October 1871

In the month when the shadows run long, my father and the other men rode away toward the rising sun to make peace with the U.S. Army. That evening I lay snugly between my mother, two sisters, and infant brother.

When it turned midnight, we were awakened by the sound of gunshots. There were screams everywhere. My mother and sisters ran for their lives. I scrambled under a clump of bushes and waited for the terror to end. But the full moon rose over the peaks, and its bright light revealed my hiding place. A strange man spotted me. He snatched me up by the arm and bound me with rope. I stood terrified and watched my village burn.

Before that horrible night, I had never seen a horse. Nor had I ever seen a dead person. That night I saw both. That night I cried.

Pima Woman

The Pima and Yavapai had been enemies before the white people came. The U.S. Army did nothing to stop the Pima from attacking the Yavapai. In fact, the army hired many Pima men to work as scouts and hunters to find those who refused to sign peace treaties and move onto the reservations.

The Trek over the Hot Desert

October 1871

I learned that my captors were the Pima—longtime enemy of my people. A Pima warrior lifted me upon a horse, and we rode for two days over the hot Arizona desert. When we reached their village, I was given pumpkin, corn, and horsemeat to eat, but I could not stomach these. Perhaps it was because I had never tasted these foods before. Perhaps it was because I was too scared.

There were close to four hundred men, women, and children in the village. I was afraid they might kill me and therefore resolved to do whatever I could to please them. During this time, the Pima were very kind to me.

On the third day of my captivity, I saw several Pima pointing at me. Some laughed. Others looked sad when my eyes met theirs. My captors painted their faces and began their war dance. The whole village danced around me. The men threatened me with spears and war clubs. The women threw dirty rags, and the children spat. An enemy captive was quite a prize—even if it was a mere sobbing child.

Everyone I knew and loved was gone. The Pima gave me a new name, Hejelweiikan, which means, "left alone."

The Storeroom

Mid-November 1871

After a week with the Pima, I was taken away to be sold as a slave. We stopped at a house, where I was led into a dark storeroom. There was a boy in the room the same size as myself. His eyes would not leave mine. When I kicked my foot up, he did the same. I raised my arm, and he followed. I turned my head, and his gaze stayed on me. I made a face, and he imitated the move. I was so angry at this boy that I jumped up, ready to fight. At that very moment, he disappeared.

Years later, I realized the boy who had mimicked me was a mirror—the true reflection of me.

Wassaja in Apache Regalia

This photo was taken a year after Wassaja was captured by the Pima. He no doubt posed in this garb as Wassaja still thought of himself as Apache.

Carlo Gentile

Carlos Montezuma's (Wassaja's) adoptive father Carlo Gentile. Many of the photographs in this book were taken by Gentile.

Pima Captor

The man in the picture is believed to be one of Wassaja's captors wearing the coat he bought with the money from the boy's sale. African American slavery had been abolished in the United States after the Civil War but the enslavement of native people remained. Mexican-Americans and Anglo-Americans used Native American slaves to work in mines. Some were forced into manual labor or domestic service. Many of these Native American slaves were taken during raids.

The Transaction
Mid-November 1871

The Pima tried to trade me for a horse but were unsuccessful. I was dragged through the town until they met a man who called himself Mr. Carlo Gentile.

While I could not understand what any of the other men said, I knew Mr. Gentile's words sounded different. It was only later that I learned he had come to America from Italy and crossed the vast Atlantic Ocean for adventure, art, and gold.

Mr. Gentile carried a small wooden box that flashed light into people's eyes. I thought the box was a gun, and it frightened me until I learned of its magic. Why, it could take a person's face off without hurting them and put it on a white leaf. He called his box a camera.

Mr. Gentile had no need for a dirty little boy, but he paid thirty silver dollars for me anyway and bought my life. One of my captors purchased a coat with the money, and Mr. Gentile took a picture of him.

Comforted to Some Degree

Mid-November 1871

Mr. Gentile's first challenge as my new parent was to feed me. I grabbed some meat but quickly dropped it because of the taste of onion. Next, I was given beans. I nibbled on them for a bit. They were good. Then I dipped my hands into the bowl and carried a handful of beans to my mouth. Before I finished, I was covered from head to toe in beans.

The next morning, Mr. Gentile dunked me into the town well and gave me a bath. Then he cut my long hair and fitted me for shoes, socks, long shirts, and pants. I was becoming "civilized."

I cried all the time, and Mr. Gentile tried to comfort me. He heard of a man who owned two young Indian girls and thought it might help if I visited them.

Wassaja and His Two Sisters
This picture was taken a few weeks after the capture of Wassaja and his sisters, Cow-wow-se-puchia and the elder, Ho-lac-ca.

We traveled 50 miles (80 kilometers) in a horse and wagon to meet with the girls. They waited for us in front of a white farmhouse. Both wore colored dresses and sunbonnets, and I did not recognize them. But they shouted my name, "Wassaja!"

Behold! They were my two sisters. I will never forget that day! We held hands and talked about the nice things we received. But thoughts of our parents and of our being prisoners forever crushed our spirits.

Mr. Gentile took a picture of us.

After two or three more visits, we left my sisters behind and I never saw them again.

The Name I Now Bear

Mid-November 1871

I could not speak English, and Mr. Gentile knew none of my language. But I soon learned that I could feel safe with my new father. I knew I would not be treated as a slave.

Mr. Gentile was a religious man and as his new son, I was baptized. I was also given a new name to fit my new life. My first name, Carlos, was after Mr. Gentile's own name—Carlo. And, my last name, Montezuma, was taken from the Montezuma ruins near my boyhood home. I would never forget *Wassaja*, as my real name. Its meaning, "beckoning," suits me even as a man.

Montezuma Ruins

Anglo-American settlers once believed that these ruins were the remains of a castle built by the Aztec emperor, Moctezuma (also called Montezuma). These ruins are actually prehistoric dwellings made by the Sinagua people during the twelfth century.

Halls of Montezuma

Carlo Gentile took many pictures when he traveled. The child wearing a hat in the middle of the picture is believed to be young Carlos Montezuma.

Iron Horses

The rest of 1871 and into 1872

Mr. Gentile's vagabond heart searched for new places to visit. He spoke of an iron horse that would take us anywhere we wanted. We stood on a wood platform and waited for the iron horse to arrive. Others also waited, and I could not understand how we could all fit on its back.

When a whistle blew, everyone craned their necks and yelled, "It's here, it's here." I was amazed—the sound was louder than an Apache war whoop. I had never seen a horse like this. It looked like a large arm pulling wheels that spat out hot, curling, dark smoke. I knew that nothing living was that strong and this great monster must eat horses to move as it did.

The iron horse took us across the land much faster than any horse and wagon ever could. We traveled to Denver in the West; Washington, D.C., and New York in the East; south to Florida; and north to Canada. All the while, Mr. Gentile took pictures of the people and the countryside.

Buffalo Bill (second from left) and Texas Jack (right)

This photo shows the cast of the play The Scouts of the Prairie, And Red Deviltry As It Is!

Carlos Montezuma Posing with Actor Alessandro Salvini

Alessandro Salvini was an actor and friend of Carlo Gentile. Most Native American children had their hair cut as a part of "Americanizing" them into Anglo-American society. To some Native Americans, cutting one's hair had spiritual meaning, such as mourning the death of a loved one. Gentile allowed Carlos to keep his hair long at times.

Buffalo Bill's Wild West Show

November 1872

In the midst of our travels, we stopped in Chicago. Mr. Gentile had the good fortune of meeting the legendary scouts of the American West—Buffalo Bill Cody and Texas Jack. These men were hired to act in the stage production *The Scouts of the Prairie, And Red Deviltry As It Is!*

Being the only native around, I was hired. I quickly became the young Apache captive, Azteka, child of Cochise. It was my job to race through the aisles and threaten another actor with my arrows and shouts.

My performance delighted the crowds. It was standing room only at the opera house!

Mr. Gentile was hired to take souvenir pictures, or *carte-de-visites*, for everyone. After three weeks, we left the famous scouts and other actors behind. Mr. Gentile was sure new adventures awaited us.

Circumstances Cast My Lot in Eastern Civilization

Settling Down in 1872

I had grown comfortable with my new father. In many ways, we were both strangers in this land.

Mr. Gentile found that all the traveling was hard on me. After almost a year together, we settled in Chicago. It was there that I was enrolled in my first public school.

From time to time, Mr. Gentile would leave me behind with friends while he continued on his trips.

He was a photographer, after all, and needed to take pictures that would sell in his photo art studio. Nevertheless, his friends were kind and took great care of me.

I made friends of my own. I also found a job as a newsboy. Early on Sunday mornings, I was to separate and deliver two newspapers, the *Times* and the *Tribune*. Because I was not able to read, I couldn't tell the difference between the two papers, so my friends would help.

From our early morning jobs, my friends and I would walk to Sunday school. It was difficult for me to understand what was preached for I had not yet mastered the white man's tongue, but the music moved me. I looked forward to each meeting just to hear the people sing.

Preacher's Family
1875 through 1889

When I was eleven years old, Mr. Gentile's photo art studio burned to ashes and his finances were in ruin. Mr. Gentile was forced to leave me behind with a preacher's family while he rebuilt his career. I worked alongside the preacher's children. We plowed the fields in the summer and did winter chores before and after school. There was little free time, but I was treated kindly.

Mr. Gentile wrote to me often. He concerned himself over my health, as well as my mind and education. He took great pride in me, and some would think that he spoiled me. As any parent, he dreamed of great things for me. Even my teachers took a special interest in me. I caught on and worked hard, and my teachers delighted in my instruction. By the time I was fourteen, I had graduated from high school and was then accepted to the University of Illinois. Chemistry was my specialty, and I did well enough to graduate from the university at seventeen. I was soon accepted at the Chicago Medical College.

Though scholarships paid for my schooling, I needed money to live. So I swept floors and washed windows for warm meals and a bed at night. In the summer, I followed the plow. After five years, I finally became a doctor.

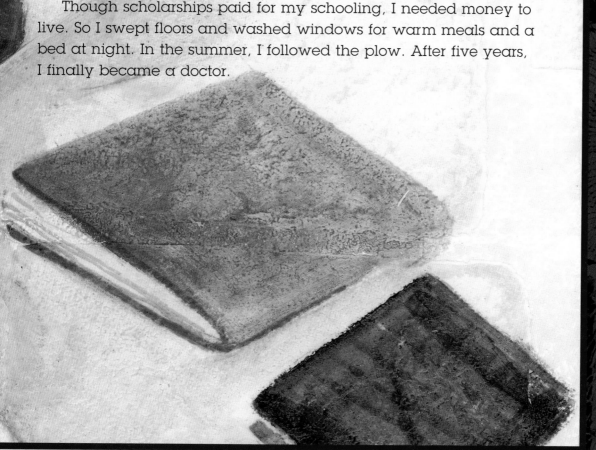

Carlos Montezuma at Eight

Anglo Americans and immigrant European boys sometimes taunted young Carlos because of his heritage. Gentile did not believe in violence but did teach his son to defend himself. But little Carlos's most important defense was not his good punch but rather the beginnings of a great education.

Carlos Montezuma as a Teenager

When Carlos Montezuma was fourteen years old he was accepted at the University of Illinois. He graduated from college at the age of seventeen. A year later, he entered the Chicago Medical College at Northwestern University. Few students of that day accomplished as much at such an early age.

The "Beckoning" of My Family

1893 through 1899

While I worked as a doctor, I began to search for my lost family. I learned that when my sisters were still young, they were taken to Sonora, Mexico. They grew up and eventually married and had children of their own. Both my sisters died before I ever had a chance to see them again. I found their children and formed close bonds with them instead.

But what of the others? My father, mother, and infant brother? Thirty years after the horrible midnight massacre, I finally learned the truth.

My father was on his way back from the peace mission when he heard of the massacre. Fearing more trouble, he went to San Carlos Reservation, where he was promised protection by the U.S. soldiers.

My mother managed to grab my infant brother and run to safety during the raid. My brother was too young and died of exposure several weeks later. Somehow my mother found her way to San Carlos Reservation, where she joined my father.

Months after the raid, my mother was approached by an Indian runner who had seen me traveling with Mr. Gentile. She was determined to reach me, but to do so, she had to travel 150 miles (242 km) over the roughest and most dangerous terrain of Arizona. But a mother's heart knows no fear. She went to the army to secure a pass that would permit her to go outside the reservation. They refused. My mother left anyway. Her body was found in a rugged canyon with the bullet from a Fort Apache scout. My father was brokenhearted when he learned of her death. He lived at San Carlos Reservation until he died of a fever.

PRESCOTT

CAMP DATE CREEK

ARIZ

Gila River

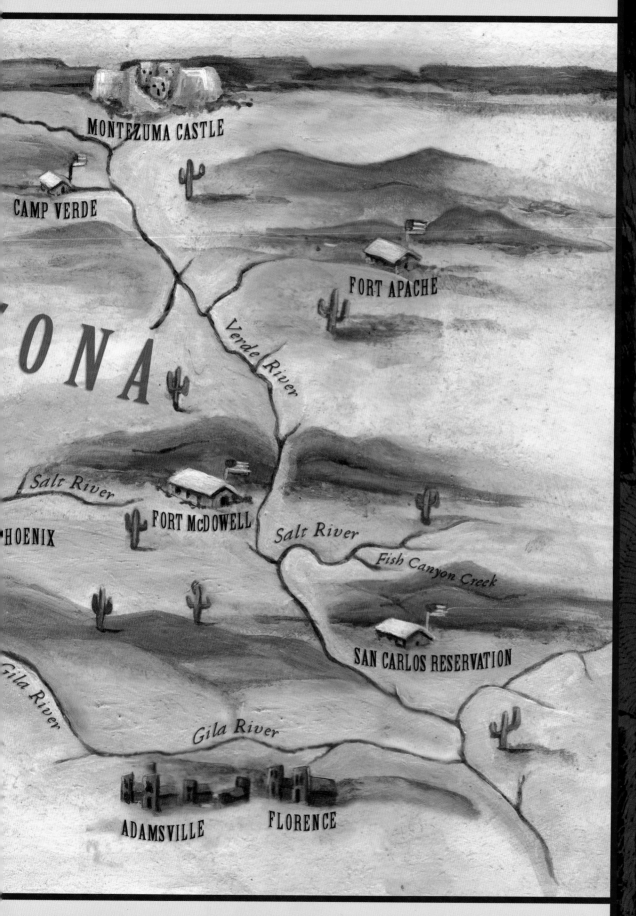

MONTEZUMA CASTLE

CAMP VERDE

ZONA

Verde River

FORT APACHE

Salt River

FORT McDOWELL

Salt River

HOENIX

Fish Canyon Creek

Gila River

SAN CARLOS RESERVATION

Gila River

ADAMSVILLE   FLORENCE

Yavapai Captives at Camp Verde, Arizona

In February 1875, more than a thousand Native Americans were forcibly moved through 180 miles (290 km) of rough terrain from Camp Verde (Rio Verde Agency) to San Carlos Reservation. The Native Americans carried their bags, children, and sometimes even their elders on their backs as they dragged themselves over hills and through streams in the bitter cold and snow. Hundreds died on the march.

Yavapai Chief at Camp Date Creek, Arizona

Yavapai chief Ahoochykahmah wears a U.S. Army coat. The chief died in 1874 while a prisoner of the U.S. Army. The army had promised food and housing to Yavapai who came to the reservation, but the promises were not kept. Disease and poor treatment killed many Yavapai who remained on the reservation.

Comfort, 1905

Now I find myself in Chicago, where I practice my profession as a doctor. I also teach at the College of Physicians and Surgeons, the Post Graduate Medical College, and the Chicago Hospital College of Medicine.

Friend, all was not lost. Through good friends and by my own personal effort in the conflict of life, I have experienced what life means.

After so many years, my heart continues to beckon me to help my people. I write and work for them and am forever dedicated to their interests.

Sincerely yours,
Carlos Montezuma, MD
"Wassaja," American Indian

Carlos Montezuma as a Doctor

Only a few months out of medical school, Carlos Montezuma began work as a reservation doctor. The government's view of his people offended him. Once-proud men and women were treated as children with no concern for their mind, spirit, or culture. Dr. Montezuma worked hard to change the government's Native American policy and close down the Office of Indian Affairs. He gave lectures and published a newsletter, Wassaja, which focused on civil rights for Native American people. All the while, Dr. Montezuma maintained his medical practice and research as well as his teaching schedule at three Chicago medical schools.

Dr. Montezuma —The Activist

What can I get? is a fatal question for a man ... the true query of a man, even one who would get much is, "what can I give."
—*Dr. Carlos Montezuma*

The world of the Native Americans changed radically over the course of Dr. Montezuma's life. In the 1860's, Native Americans had not yet been fully suppressed by the U.S. Army. Within a short ten years, Native Americans were forced to move from their homelands and onto reservations. The reservations at that time were more like prisons than homes. They were rife with greed and mismanagement. The Office of Indian Affairs, which managed the reservations, was often staffed by culturally ignorant and prejudicial government officials.

Having been brought up in an urban area, Carlos Montezuma did not know much about the struggle of the Native Americans on the reservations—all he knew was that he wanted to do something to help his people. An influential friend recommended Dr. Montezuma, fresh out of medical school, to the Office of Indian Affairs. In 1889 Montezuma was hired to work as a physician at Fort Stevenson. He quickly witnessed the wretched living conditions of the people on the reservations. These experiences changed Dr. Montezuma's life forever.

He concluded that the future of the Native American was bleak unless there were to be dramatic change. He saw those living on the reservations as living in squalor and fear. Dr. Montezuma believed that they needed opportunities to grow, just as he had, so they would flourish in their new society. That could only happen through education and by receiving U.S. citizenship.

To accomplish his lofty goals, Dr. Montezuma believed that he must be a model of hope for his people, so he gave up the security of his government job and struck out on his own.

The gravity of his people's future caused the doctor to call the Office of Indian Affairs and the reservations "un-American institutions." His most famous speech, "Let my people go ...."* was read on the U.S Senate floor in 1916:

"As their children ... can we dare stay back, hide ourselves and be dumb at this hour, when we see our race abused, misused and driven back to its doom? If this be not so, then let whatever loyalty and racial pride be in you awaken and manifest itself in this greatest movement of 'Let My People Go!'

... In behalf of our people, with the spirit of Moses, I ask this—THE UNITED STATES OF AMERICA—"LET MY PEOPLE GO."

Dr. Montezuma was never a reservation Indian. He chose to live in a "white" world, married a Romanian woman, and placed his successful medical practice in Chicago. In so doing, he sought to be an example for both Anglo-Americans and Native Americans. He was not without enemies. The managers from the Office of Indian Affairs referred to him as a troublemaker. Eventually, the Federal Bureau of Investigation (FBI), then known as the Department of Justice, accused Montezuma of producing literature intended to incite disloyalty to the United States among Native Americans. Still, Dr. Montezuma would not stop shouting out. He became the American Indian's strongest voice.

The last twelve years of Dr. Montezuma's life were directed specifically to fighting for his ancestral people's right to remain on their homeland. Up until his death, he successfully lobbied the government to honor their original treaties with the Yavapai.

Dr. Montezuma dedicated his life to helping others, but no one could help him when he was stricken with tuberculosis. After being diagnosed, he left Chicago and moved to his childhood home in the Arizona mountains.

In January 1923, Dr. Montezuma's life came full circle. His body was found in an oo-wah wearing nothing more than a breechcloth. Once again and forever, he became Wassaja.

Just one year after Dr. Montezuma's death, Congress passed the Indian Citizenship Act of 1924, which established all Native Americans as citizens of the United States.

Bibliography

A Note on Use of Sources

The following explains how I reconstructed and chronicled Dr. Carlos Montezuma's life. The bibliography provides publishing data. Much of the text within this book is based on the original letter Dr. Montezuma sent to Professor Holmes in 1905. The letter is stored at the Smithsonian Institution, National Anthropological Archives.

I reconstructed the accounts of Montezuma's early life mainly from an interview he gave in 1921 to writer, N. M. Clark. The article, "Dr. Montezuma, Apache Warrior in Two Worlds," was eventually printed in the *Magazine of Western History*. The information on Montezuma's later life came from "The Papers of Carlos Montezuma." These nineteen microfiche reels from Scholarly Resources are located in various depositories around the nation. The versions I used are housed at the Southwest Museum of the American Indian in Los Angeles. Montezuma; his wife, Maria Keller Montezuma Moore; and his attorney, James W. Latimer, originally accumulated the information provided within the papers. The archives are a collection of Montezuma's letters, correspondence, articles, speeches, self-published newspapers, pamphlets—and even some bills for copper piping. These collections also include a copy of the congressional papers, which documents Montezuma's historic pleas of "Let my people go" read on the U.S. Senate floor.

Further research for this book was gleaned from Smithsonian Institution anthropologist Cesare Marino's book, *The Remarkable Carlo Gentile: Italian Photographer of the American Frontier*. Marino's documentation covers the early life, relationship, and photos of Carlo Gentile and Carlos Montezuma. A timeline and details about Montezuma's life and his relationship with the Yavapai is in historian Peter Iverson's book, *Carlos Montezuma and the Changing World of the American Indians*. An additional source of details, written and researched within historical contexts, is Leon Speroff's book, *Carlos Montezuma, M.D: A Yavapai American Hero*.

Chaudhuri, Jonodev Osceola. *The Yavapai of Fort McDowell: An Outline of the History and Culture of a Community*. Mesa, AZ: Mead Publishing, 1995.

Clark, N. M. "Dr. Montezuma, Apache Warrior in Two Worlds." *Montana: Magazine of Western History* 23 (1973): 56–65.

Gill, Sam D., and Irene F. Sullivan. *Dictionary of Native American Mythology*. New York: Oxford University Press, 1992.

Hohler, Johanne Stranberg, ed. *The Papers of Carlos Montezuma 1892–1937*. Madison: State Historical Society of Wisconsin, 1975.

Iverson, Peter. *Carlos Montezuma and the Changing World of the American Indians*. Albuquerque: University of New Mexico Press, 1982.

Josephy, Alvin M., Jr. *500 Nations, An Illustrated History of the Native American Indians*. New York: Alfred A. Knopf, 1994.

Larner, John Williams, Jr., ed. *The Papers of Carlos Montezuma*. Wilmington, DE: Scholarly Resources, 1987.

Marino, Cesare. *The Remarkable Carlo Gentile: Italian Photographer of the American Frontier*. Nevada City, CA: Carl Mautz Publishing, 1998.

Montezuma, Carlos. "A Review of Commissioner Leupp's Interview in the *New York Daily Tribune*, April 9, 1905, on the Future of Our Indians." *To-morrow*. Privately printed by Carlos Montezuma, M.D., 1905.

———. "An Apache Protest." *Quarterly Journal of the Society of American Indians* 7, no. 1, (1919), 294–299.

———. "From an Apache Camp to a Chicago Medical College: The Story of Carlos Montezuma's Life as Told by Himself." *Red Man* 8, no. 9 (1888), 3–6.

———. "Indian Men Are Not Freaks." *To-morrow*. Privately printed by Carlos Montezuma, M.D., 1905.

———. "Justice to the Indian." *To-morrow*. Privately printed by Carlos Montezuma, M.D., 1905.

———. "Life, Liberty & Citizenship." *To-morrow*. Privately printed by Carlos Montezuma, M.D., 1905.

———. "Light on the Indian Situation." *Quarterly Journal of the Society of American Indians* 1, no. 1 (1913), 50–55.

———. "On the Future of Our Indians." *To-morrow*. Privately printed by Carlos Montezuma, M.D., 1905.

———. "Philanthropy of the Indian Department." *To-morrow*. Privately printed by Carlos Montezuma, M.D., 1905.

———. "What Indians Must Do." *Quarterly Journal of the Society of American Indians* 2, no. 4 (1914), 294–299.

Spier, Leslie. *Yuman Tribes of the Gila River*. New York: Dover Publications, 1978.

Taylor, Colin F., ed. *The Native Americans, the Indigenous People of North America*. New York: Smithmark Publ., 1991.

Thorne, Kate Roland. *Yavapai: The People of the Red Rocks— The People of the Sun*. Sedona, AZ: Thorne Enterprises Publications, 1995.

Waterstrat, Elaine. *Hoomothya's Long Journey, 1865–1897. The True Story of a Yavapai Indian*. Fountain Hills, AZ: Mount McDowell Press, 1998.

Whiteford, Andrew Hunter. *Southwestern Indian Baskets: Their History and Their Makers*. Santa Fe, NM: School of American Research Press, 1988.

Letters to Montezuma

*Department of the Interior—Office of Indian Affairs (Letter to Montezuma from Commissioner). June 28, 1887.

Morgan, Thomas J. to Carlos Montezuma, August 3, 1889. Delaware: Scholarly Resources, 1984.

Morgan, Thomas J. to Carlos Montezuma, May 14, 1890. Delaware: Scholarly Resources, 1984.

Morgan, Thomas J. to Carlos Montezuma, June 27, 1890. Delaware: Scholarly Resources, 1984.

Morgan, Thomas J. to Carlos Montezuma, July 1, 1890. Delaware: Scholarly Resources, 1984.

Pratt, R. H., Papers. Beinecke Library Yale University.

Pratt, R. H. to Carlos Montezuma, February 25, 1888. Delaware: Scholarly Resources, 1984.

Pratt, R. H. to Carlos Montezuma, March 28, 1888. Delaware: Scholarly Resources, 1984.

Pratt, R. H. to Carlos Montezuma, July 21, 1890. Delaware: Scholarly Resources, 1984.

Letters from Carlos Montezuma

Montezuma, Carlos. "Letter to Professor William H. Holmes." (National Anthropological Archives, Smithsonian Institution, Washington, DC), 1905.

Montezuma, Carlos. "Letter to President Theodore Roosevelt, January 29, 1904." Delaware: Scholarly Resources, 1984.

Montezuma, Carlos to Thomas J. Morgan, May 14, 1890. Delaware: Scholarly Resources, 1984.

Montezuma, Carlos to Thomas J. Morgan, June 27, 1890. Delaware: Scholarly Resources, 1984.

Websites

Answers.com "Carlos Montezuma." *answers.com*. 2001. http://www.answers.com/topic/montezuma-carlos (March 1, 2007).

Fort Mcdowell Yavapai Nation. "Yavapai History." *fortmcdowell.org*. N.d. http://www.fortmcdowell.org/ History%20&%20Cultural.htm (February 26, 2007).

Home.epix.net. "Carlos Montezuma and the Carlisle Indian Industrial School." *home.epix.net*. N.d. http://home.epix.net,/~landis/montezuma.htm (March, 2007).

Jacobs, James Q. "Water Politics and the History of the Fort McDowell Indian Community." *jqjacobs.net*. 2000. http://www.jqjacobs.net/southwest/fort_mcdowell.html (February, 26, 2007).

Spack, Ruth. "Dis/engagement Zitkala-Sa's Letters to Carlos Montezuma, 1901–1902." *MELUS*, Spring 2001, 1–15.

U.S. National Library of Medicine. "If You Knew the Conditions" . . . Health Care to the Native Americans: An Exhibit at the National Library of Medicine 15 April -1994-31." *nlm.nih.gov*. April 20, 1998. http://www.nlm.nih.gov/ exhibition/if_you_knew/if_you_knew_10.html (March 2007).

Speeches

Congressional Record-Sixty-fourth Congress, First Session. "*Let My People Go*" Washington, DC, 8,888–8,891.

Montezuma, Carlos. "*The Indian of Tomorrow*." Chicago: National Women's Christian Temperance Union, 1888.

———. "*Let My People Go*." Annual Conference of the Society of American Indians at Lawrence, Kansas, September 30, 1915.

———. "*The World in Chicago*," Speech, Coliseum, Chicago, May 13, 1913.

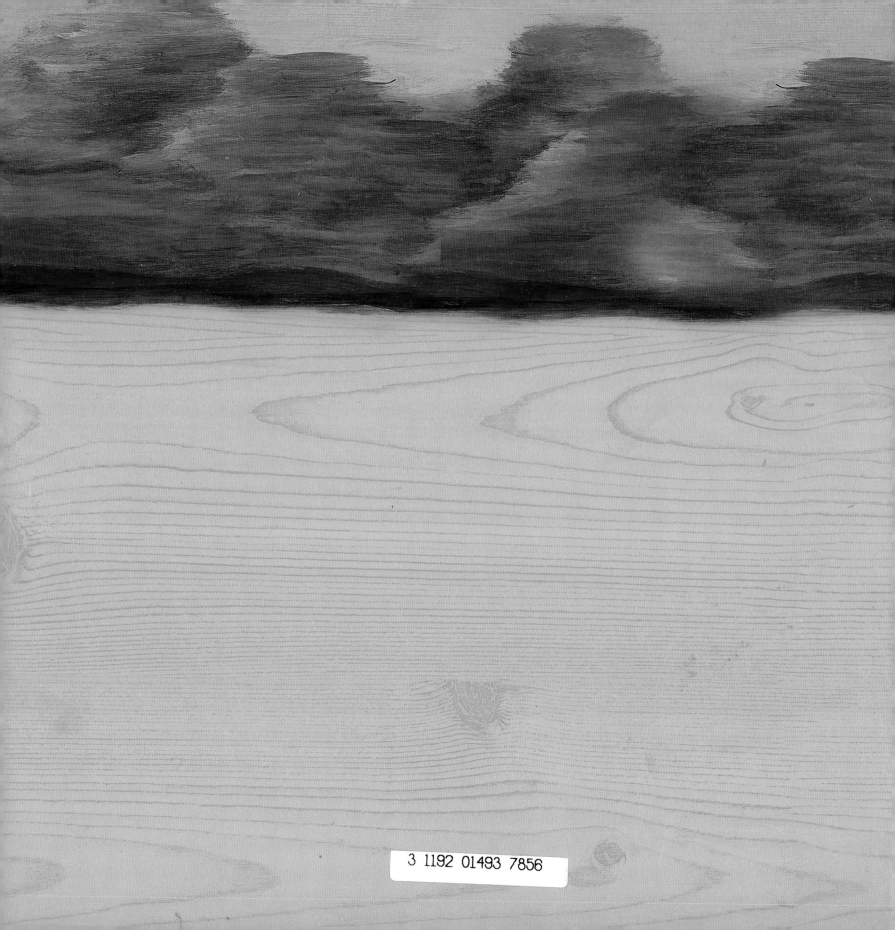